Doing Good

Sola Olukoya

Published by **Treasure Projects**
ISBN: 978-978-598-8
Printed in Nigeria

Published & Designed by

TREASURE PROJECTS

Printing with a difference

P O Box 8384 Wuse, Zone 3, Abuja
+234 703 472 4872

Edited By: Spotless
+234 906 130 1049

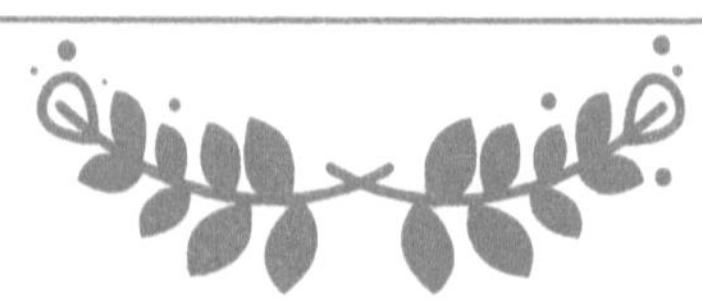

Dedication

To my Lord and personal savior, who has taught and helped me to keep doing good.

To RCCG Jesus Embassy brethren both old and young. I celebrate you all.

Acknowledgment

I want to acknowledge with honor, love and gratitude thos[e] whom God has brought through my paths to be a blessin[g] to me, and all who I have been able to be a blessing to. If I must mention names or give examples it will be as if I a[m] blowing my trumpet because all glory belongs to God.

I particularly celebrate the members of RCCG Jesus Embass[y] and most especially the working team, whom I was able to pou[r] out myself unto. For your labour, your service, your obedienc[e] love, patience, trust, belief and honoring God in me.

To my lovely wife, my joy of inestimable value, my Queen an[d] lover of my soul and the lovely spiritual and biological childre[n] that God has given unto us. I celebrate you all.

Thanks for your labour of love and your understanding with m[e] despite my busy schedule, God bless you richly.

Contents

Dedication... i

Acknowledgment.. ii

Preface... iv

Introduction.. vi

Chapter 1

Doing Good.. 1-6

Chapter 2

You can never go wrong doing good.........................10-11

Chapter 3

Steps in doing good.......................................15-19

Chapter 4

Benefits of Helping.......................................23-24

Chapter 5

What do I have to gain....................................28-32

Chapter 6

Doing good by Salvation...................................36

Chapter 7

Doing good by Soul Winning................................40-42

Chapter 8

Life Is Not About Duration But Donation...................46-49

20 Scriptures on Doing Good.............................50-52

Preface

Jesus encourages us to do good both to the body and sou
of men; to the latter, by preaching the Gospel to them
and to the former, by curing all their diseases, o
whatsoever sort: he did what none of Adam's sons could do, fo
there is none of them that does good, no not one, Romans 3:1
he was good himself, essentially and naturally good, an
therefore he did good, and he did nothing but good: he knev
no sin, he did none, nor could any be found in him; and h
always did good, that which was according to the will of Goo
and well pleasing in his sight; and without him no good is done
even by his own people; they have all the grace and strengt
from him, by which they perform the good things they do: he i
the reverse of Satan, who goes about doing all the mischief h
can; and he is to be imitated by his followers, who, as they hav
opportunity, should do good to all men, especially to th
household of faith.

Gal 6:10 KJV

> *As we have therefore opportunity, let us d
> good unto all men, especially unto ther
> who are of the household of faith*

Throughout the centuries, Christians have give
generously and sacrificially for the cause of the Gospe
Christians have funded schools, charity homes, and hospitals
Christians have given time and treasure to rebuild cities afte

ods and fires. Christians have given faithfully to their local urches, to missionaries, to neighbors in need, and have given nsistently in ways that others will never know. Following the ad of our Savior who gave all on our behalf, Christians are a ving people. I want to encourage you today not to give up. **alatians 6:9 says**

> *Let us not become weary in doing good,*
> *for at the proper time we will reap a*
> *harvest if we do not give up.*

Today, I pray that neither you nor I will give up, but we will ap the rewards in the proper time if we faint not. You can ver go wrong in doing good. I know that many people would ve offended you, broken your heart and make you feel bad. he thing that is certain is that my God will surely heal your oken heart, remember all your good works and reward you cordingly.

Introduction

Are you doing good? May be you are doing good life financially or physically or in other ways, b are you really doing good? I'm not asking if yc are doing great things in the world, your business, career. I'm not even asking if you are good persona in your relationship with people. I'm asking if you a doing good according to biblically injunctions. Are yc doing good in Christ? Are you doing good with Goc plan for your life? Are you doing good for eterni sake?

These are the questions that you need to sit dow as a person to provide appropriate answers to in yo own interest. The bible says know yea not yourse except yea be reprobate. The truth is that eve individual can attest to it if he or she is doing good not. I will want you to think deeply about this ar make amends as soon as possible.

Chapter One

Doing Good

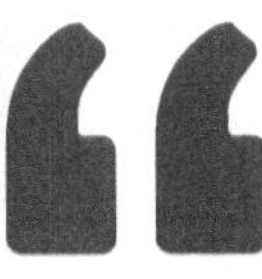

Keep doing good to people...
maybe it'll be unappreciated,
unreciprocated, or ignored,
but spread the love anyway.
Your reward is at the corner

-Sola Olukoya- 

esus Christ our perfect example was doing good throughout hi life time, there is no portion in the scripture where it wa recorded that Jesus Christ was doing bad or engage in an terrible act of wickedness, rather, Jesus is always moved wit compassion for His people and His thought is only on how to: d them good, liberate them, deliver his people, healing them and hov to solve their imminent problems by extending his good hands c grace unto them.

The major assignment of Jesus Christ during his life time ministr was to look at his children and attend to their pressing needs, som of the good deeds of Jesus are: he raised the deadLazarus, he heale the woman with issue of blood, he healed the man that was sick fo thirty eight years, he healed the mad man of Gadarenes, he heale Bartimeaus the blind man, he still the storm, and several other goo things were done by our Lord Jesus Christ. His desire is to see hi children doing same as long as they are here on earth in order t secure his ever abiding presence.

Acts 10:38 KJV

How God anointed Jesus of Nazareth with the Holy Ghost and with power: who went about doing good, and healing all that were oppressed of the devil; for God was with him.

Doing good is an upright, moral and godly way of life; you ca decide to be a philanthropy. You can☐t lose your reward. You ma also decide to go out for rigorous evangelism. You can even be sourc of livelihood for as many that are thinking of suicide. Your own ma even be to give hope for the hopeless. That child that has droppe out of school can resume the next term when you pick him up an back him up. All these are simply doing good.
Doing good is synonymous to morally excellent; virtuous

hteous; pious, satisfactory in quality, quantity, or degree of high
ality; excellent, right; proper; fit, well-behaved, kind, beneficent, or
endly, having admirable, pleasing, superior, or positive qualities;
t negative, bad, or mediocre. Each time you demonstrate this
havior it is counted unto you as doing something good.

It is the will of God that you must go about doing good. Doing
od is a seed just as you plant a seed in the soil and it is expected to
rminate someday. Doing good is fulfilling God's will for your life.
hat is your business judging others? What makes you not to impact
es? Those adamic natures will disappear if you keep doing good.
u are now a different breed, the DNA of Jesus has taken over your
. Every power, grace, strength in Jesus has been released into you
cause you carry his DNA.

Jeremiah 17:9-10 KJV
The heart is deceitful above all t h i n g s ,   a n d
desperately wicked: who can know it? I the Lord search
the heart, I try the reins, even to give every man
according to his ways, and according to the fruit of his
doings.

Every average man's heart is deceitful and is not spirit filled, he
desperately wicked and self-centered. What is the state of your
art? To do good have lots to do with your state of heart, the bible
ys guide your heart with all diligence for out it are the issues of life.
e lords knows the state of our heart, he searches the reins of heart,
ere is always a reward for every good we do, likewise, there is
ward for every bad deeds we engage in, why can't we then make
our minds to rather do good instead of doing otherwise.

Ephesians 6:7-8 KJV
With good will doing service, as to the Lord, and not to
men: Knowing that whatsoever good thing any man doeth,

When you are doing good forget about reward, forget abo[ut] human praise, and forget about people taking note of you. Know[ing] fully well that it is unto the Lord. He knows what to package for yo[u] reward; He knows the appropriate timing for your rewards to co[me] in. It is very certain that you can't lose your rewards if you faint n[ot,] God is not mocked, whatsoever a man sows, the same he shall reap[.]

Hebrews 11:6 KJV
But without faith it is impossible to please him : for he that cometh to God must believe that he is, and that he is a rewarder of them that diligently seek him.

If God is the greatest rewarder then you can be rest assure[d] that he will greatly reward you beyond what any man can offer you.

You can never sow into grace without receiving from Go[d.] Whenever my father in the Lord comes to town, I see it as [an] opportunity to sow into his life. I keep sowing into the life of [a] father and mother in the Lord and I keep increasing. Giving someo[ne] a huge hug and a smile can restore hope and life. I will like to cite th[is] example as a case study, a man who was tired going from house [to] house for evangelism and was about to give up when God told him [to] visit one house more, as he entered the house a man was about [to] commit suicide, but through his obedience to the leading of God, th[e] man's life was savaged. Today, he is bubbling in the Lord. The impa[ct] we make while doing good will always go far beyond our lives a[nd] understanding. People may easily forget what you did but they w[ill] never forget the impact your seed played in their lives.

The expectations of God from us as His children after o[ur] salvation and baptism, is more than what we think. He expects us [to]

ntinue doing good. To whom much is given, much shall be
quired; He has saved us, redeemed us, and liberated us from all
anners of terrible experiences and challenges. He wants us to
ciprocate this love by continually doing good. Therefore, stop
mplaining, and see whatsoever you do as doing it as unto the Lord.
od alone is the rewarder of your destiny. Don't let every opportunity
 do good pass you bye.

song writer wrote; "

Everywhere He went, He was doing good
Almighty healer, He healed the leper
When the cripple saw Him They started walking
Even today my Lord was doing good

The most painful thing with us nowadays Christians is the fact
at we are making mockery of ourselves and the assignment God
as given unto us as believers. There are so many needy around us
nd all over, if only we can tune our spirit open our eyes, and connect
 God in the spirit and also allow Him to lead us aright. We will help
ts of these destinies that are wasting away and the under privilege
nd fulfillment in life, when we begin to operate as God expects from
.

What is the opposite of good? ill, bad, poor, wickedness, sin, or
vil and the like. Anytime we don't do good, it means we are doing
therwise by operating below the expectations of God from us as His
ildren and we are going against the will of God. We need to make
is word of God our life style and follow the example of our Lord.
cts 10:38 KJV

How God anointed Jesus of Nazareth with the Holy
Ghost and with power: who went about doing good,
and healing all that were oppressed of the devil; for
God was with him.

If Jesus is inside of you, you can do good. Jesus said in
John 15:4-5 KJV

> *Abide in me, and I in you. As the branch cannot bear fruit of itself, except it abide in the vine; no more can ye, except ye abide in me. I am the vine, ye are the branches: He that abideth in me, and I in him, the same bringeth forth much fruit: for without me ye can do nothing.*

By doing good you are proclaiming the gospel and Go doing good, you are meeting the needs of the needy, the helpless confused, the frustrated, the disappointed, the fatherless and widows/ widowers. The strong Adamic nature is still at work in life if you are not doing good. Have a check of your life. There need to make noise out of it. Every day you wake-up, the question you should ask yourself is, who can I be of help to to where can I be of help? who is in need of my assistance to Everything God gives unto you is for you to assist others. A l Christians are oppressed and depressed and all they need is j hug or smile. You can provide it.

Isaiah 61:1-2 KJV

> *The Spirit of the Lord God is upon me; because the Lord hath anointed me to preach good tidings unto the meek; he hath sent me to bind up the brokenhearted, to proclaim liberty to the captives, and the opening of the prison to them that are bound; To proclaim the acceptable year of the Lord , and the day of vengeance of our God; to comfort all that mourn;*

Allow and cultivate the habit of doing good. Have a g attitude towards others. Let your motive of doing good be to lory of God. Not for show off or what you are going to get in return by doing it.

1 Thessalonians 3:13 says

But ye, brethren, be not weary in well doing

Many will try to discourage you through their attitudes; do not quit. The Bible says looking unto Jesus the author and finisher of our faith. Making Him your living example and He will help you. Do not because of what anybody says change your mind about the instructions given by God.

Chapter Two

You Can Never go Wrong in Doing Good

"

If you look at your circumstance and your bank account your faith will fail you to do good, only look unto God His grace is sufficient

-Sola Olukoya-

> *Be not deceived; God is not mocked: for whatsoever*
> *a man Soweth, that shall he also reap.*

Keep doing good. You can never go wrong in doing good. obody does wrong in doing good. It is the will of the Master. It is ur attitude towards others and a way of impacting lives.
Corinthians 4:1 KJV

> *Therefore seeing we have this ministry, as we have*
> *received mercy, we faint not;*

Every man is called into this ministry of doing good. You may be scouraged, nevertheless move on. Do not allow anyone take you ut of God's way. Pleasing your maker and master is the ultimate.
John 4:4 KJV

> *Ye are of God, little children, and have overcome them:*
> *because greater is he that is in you, than he that is*
> *in the world.*

He that is in us is Jesus Christ who went about doing good. In as uch as our savior and master was going about doing good, we ould follow his foot step and see it as our duty to engage ourselves doing good.   Since Jesus was doing good anywhere He went, it ehooves on you to do same. You are no longer a natural man from e day you gave your life to Christ. You are a different being. Act fferently from others.
alatians 6:9-10 KJV

> *And let us not be weary in well doing: for in due*
> *season we shall reap, if we faint not. As we have*

*therefore opportunity, let us do good unto all men,
especially unto them who are of the household of
faith.*

To be a Christian is not easy, do not be weary or tired. Don
give up. Do not surrender to the devil and all his suggestions. Yo
may encounter back stabbing, but keep on pressing forward. Ther
must be a multiplying effect on anyone's life you impact. Go
rewards in a hundred fold. It is not expensive to do good. The mor
you dispense the more goodness you receive. Why are we not in tha
ministry? He is the one who commanded us to do so. Opportunit
comes in diverse ways and he brings it about to cause a blessing fc
you. You can never go wrong by doing good. Make sure you bles
someone anytime you have the opportunity and at all times, n
matter how small and insignificant it may be.

The scripture cannot be broken concerning the reward f
doing good. Not doing good is a sin according to:
James 4:17 KJV

*Therefore to him that knoweth to do good, and doeth
it not, to him it is sin.*

This passage is even enough to help us to continue the act c
doing good. The bible says and yea shall know the truth and th
truth shall set you free. God has done so much for us, He saved u
delivered us, gave us a warm embrace even when we were bein
rejected by loved ones. He has shown us that when we were ye
sinners, Christ died for the ungodly. We have known that doing goo
is not the matter of doing it for our friends, close relations or peopl
we love.

We can pick anybody in a degenerated state and mak
something meaningful come out of such broken life. Proof the har
of God upon your life by the lives you raise. It becomes a serious si
when God has done innumerable things for us and we refuse
extend the hand of grace unto others that are helpless.

Chapter Three

Steps to Doing Good

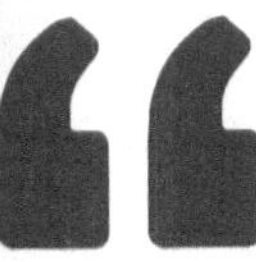

"Don't let a cruel word
escape your mouth.
Do good with your tongue,
everything is not about money"

-Sola Olukoya-

here is always time of sowing, time of waiting for the seeds to germinate and the time to reap the harvest of the seeds sown.

Genesis 8:22 KJV

While the earth remaineth, seedtime and harvest,and cold and heat, and summer and winter, and day and night shall not cease.

Luke 10:33-37 KJV

But a certain Samaritan, as he journeyed, came where he was: and when he saw him, he had compassion on him and went to him , and bound up his wounds, pouring in oil and wine, and set him on his own beast, and brought him to an inn, and took care of him. And on the morrow when he departed, he took out two pence, and gave them to the host, and said unto him, Take care of him; and whatsoever thou spendest more, when I come again, I will repay thee. Which now of these three, thinkest thou was neighbour unto him that fell among the thieves And he said, He that shewed mercy on him. Then said Jesus unto him, Go, and do thou likewise.

These were the main characters in this story.
- The miserable man
- The terrible priest
- The passing priest
- The looking Levite

The Good Samaritan-We want to look at six correspondi actions the Good Samaritan took that God expects from each a every one of us.

The first action taken by the good Samaritan was that -HE LOCATED THE NEEDY. There is need for you to go out of your comfort zone to locate the person God wants you to bless.

Mark 16:15 KJV

And he said unto them, Go ye into all the world, and preach the gospel to every creature.

This is an instruction and commandment from God unto us. Since God has given us this commandment, we are not to exercise fear in carrying out God's instruction. We are to make every tribe, every human, every race our target, there must be no reason for segregation.

2 Timothy 1:7 KJV
For God hath not given us the spirit of fear; but of power, and of love, and of a sound mind.

I have never relent in doing good. Many people used to be afraid to help people. Many people are also afraid of how to help without having the means, some believe they can't manifest. When there is mind, there will be means, nothing will be impossible for a willing mind. How willing are you to help others? Receive power and grace to be willing in Jesus name.

Another giant stride the man took was that - **HE BANDAGED HIS WOUNDS** tore his cloths just to make sure he does not lose too many blood. He was caring, he was concerned, he went extra mile just to deny himself in order to make another person feel better. How ready are you to deny yourself of your comfort and personal belongings and opportunities for the benefits of others?

This man refused to look at the negative implication of his action, he did not consider the cost implication, he was just held bent on doing good to this strange man. This man did not act like the

priest and the Levite who just passed by when they saw the man
that terribly wounded condition he was. This Good Samaritan d
not deny Christ and all the teachings he had heard on doing good.

Matthew 10:33 KJV

But whosoever shall deny me before men, him will I
also deny before my Father which is in heaven.

The Levite and the Priest denied Jesus at this point in tim
they have probably forgotten

Titus 1:16 KJV
They profess that they know God; but in works they
deny him, being abominable, and disobedient,
and unto every good work reprobate.

The third thing he did was that, **HE SHOWED KINDNESS**. The c
he poured was to sooth the wounds to make him feel better ar
relieved. It helps to reduce the pain and calm him down. He wa
neither a medical doctor nor a nurse, he has never worked in
hospital before but just because he offered himself to be used of Go
he was able to make impact in the life of this man. The wine h
poured helped to disinfect the wounds against disease, bacteria
virus and anything that can complicate then condition of this mam.

The next thing he did was that, **HE PUT THE MAN ON H
DONKEY.** This man did not mind that he will suffer stress or der
himself of his precious time. He was after the well-being of the ma
He did not consider that the man can possibly die as he takes hi
down to the hospital. His focus was on rescuing the man's life.

It was also discovered through the action of this man that, **H
WAS HOSPITABLE.** He took the man to the hospital. He did n
assume the first aid offered was enough. He took him to where h

ould get good medical aid. In today's Christianity, some professing hristians will hit a car and run away, some will even hit human being nd still abscond, some will go visiting and have no assistance to ender to the person they have gone to pay a visit. In other way ound, some are terrible to the extent that no one would be nterested in assisting them to do anything in their homes because hey are not hospitable, it is difficult for them to offer visitors a cup of old water to quench their thirst when they come visiting, to talk less bout having some gift items, or useable items to offer or give out to eople. They are miserly. This is not good enough. Change your habit nd start doing good and see how God will bless you in an nquantifiable ways.

However, under no circumstances should anybody leave your ome empty handed, whenever they come on visitation. You must lways have something to give. This is one serious virtue and hristian culture and habit we should cultivate as children of God. his has being my lifestyle since I met Christ. I always have something o offer everyone I come in contact with and I learnt this act from my piritual father and mother. The truth is that the word of God is true. ive and it shall be given unto you. The more I give, the more I have in bundance. The question is, are you hospitable? Every Christian is xpected to develop hospitality mentality.

Lastly, it was learnt by this man that, **HE FINISHED HIS TASK, ID NOT ABANDON HIM HALF WAY UNTIL THE MAN GAINED ONSCIOUSNESS** He did not do eye-service, he did not abandoned he man half way. He made sure that he did not leave the man the vay he met him. There are some people God will send your way as ou read this book, please begin to shower love on them.

N WHAT AREAS OF NEEDS CAN WE BE OF ASSISTANCE TO PEOPLE Vhat did the Samaritan take care of:-
.   Physical need.

2.	Safety Need
3.	Clothing need.
4.	Transportation need.
5.	Shelter need.
6.	Financial need.

We can decide to take care of any of these aspects in the life of person or a group of people. The more we do this, the more we continue to experience the blessings of God in every aspect of our lives too.

Chapter Four

Benefits of Helping

"

There's no greater sin than breaking a heart. Do good by mending a soul "

-Sola Olukoya-

There are lots of blessings attached to helping others whether we know them or not.

Romans 16:1-9, 17 KJV

I commend unto you Phebe our sister, which is a servant of the church which is at Cenchrea: That ye receive her in the Lord, as becometh saints, and that ye assist her in whatsoever business she hath need of you: for she hath been a succourer of many, and of myself, also Greet Priscilla and Aquila my helpers in Christ Jesus: Who have for my life laid down their own necks: unto whom not only I give thanks, but also all the church of the Gentiles. Likewise greet the church that is in their house. salute my well beloved Epaenetus, who is the first fruits of Achaia unto Christ. Greet Mary, who bestowed much labour on us. Salute Andronicus and Junia, my Kinsmen, and my fellow prisoners, who are of note among the apostles, who also were in Christ before me. Greet Amplias my beloved in the Lord. Salute Urbane, our helper in Christ, and Stachys my beloved.

When you are given to helping others, help will not be far from you too, your children and entire household will continually enjoy the goodness of God. Goodness is bound to always come back to whosoever is sold out to doing good. When you give money, money will come back to you, and mind you, it can only be better than whichever amount you have given.

When you render service, God will raise men to serve you. When you help people settle their depts. God will send financial assistance to you. When you give out clothes, shoes, cars and what have you? I tell you, they will come back in hundred folds. God does not owe you

our harvest is only dependent on what type of seed you have sown.

The following are the other benefits we enjoy as we develop the lifestyle of doing good. You shall receive power to do exploit for God. Every insurmountable mountain begins to crumble on their own. Your ministry is developed; you will no longer experience spiritual dryness. It becomes easy for you to accomplish spiritual things for the Lord. Spiritual heights become easy for you to attain, and you will always have access to the secret place of the most high. You find your calling as you will no longer major in the minor and run another man's vision. The needed helps begin to locate you. Men will begin to compete to favour you. Your allocation will begin to locate you at your location. Brethren, it is a blessing in disguise to do good on daily basis.

Chapter Five

What Do I Have To Gain?

"-Do good
-Think good
-Be good
-Act good
-Sow good"

-Sola Olukoya-

There are lots of blessings that are attached to doing good. The word of God is clear about this. The Lord promised to fight our battles if we are obedient unto His words.

odus 23:22 KJV

> *But if thou shalt indeed obey his voice, and do all that*
> *I speak; then I will be an enemy unto thine enemies,*
> *and an adversary unto thine adversaries.*

Because we were created for service.
There are blessings in serving God. Serving God attracts all und blessing.

hesians 2:10 KJV

> *"For we are God's handiwork, created in Christ Jesus*
> *to do good works, which God prepared in advance for*
> *us to do."*

It is a prove you belong to Christ.
By doing good, you begin to bear fruits unto the Lord and by doing our fruits will begin to abide in the Lord.

mans 7:4 KJV

> *"So, my brothers and sisters, you also died to the law*
> *through the body of Christ, that you might belong to*
> *another, to him who was raised from the dead, in*
> *order that we might bear fruit for God."*

Serving others is a way to serve God.
When we do it whole heartedly, there is an inheritance waiting us. There are crown of glory awaiting us for fully involved in is business. We will not lose our reward.

lossians 3:23-24

"Whatever you do, work at it with all your heart, as working for the Lord, not for human masters, since you know that you will receive an inheritance from the Lord as a reward. It is the Lord Christ you are serving" (NIV)

4.   Because you owe God everything.

Let us engage in everything that is holy and pleasing unto the Lord, God is all out to reward us for such.

Romans 12:1

"1 Therefore, I urge you, brothers and sisters, in view of God's mercy, to offer your bodies as a living sacrifice, holy and pleasing to God-this is your true and proper worship."

5.   Because it is the best use of your life.

The best way we can live our lives is by giving and using it for the Lord.

1 Corinthians 15:58

"Therefore, my dear brothers and sisters, stand firm. Let nothing move you. Always give yourselves fully to the work of the Lord, because you know that your labor in the Lord is not in vain."

6.   Because it makes life meaningful.

Serving God makes our lives more meaningful in that, it has a way of beautifying our lives. When you look keenly into the lives of servants of God, you see them radiating the glory of God.

Matthew 20: 25-28

Jesus called them together and said, "You know that the rulers of the Gentiles lord it over them, and their

high officials exercise authority over them. Not so with you. Instead, whoever wants to become great among you must be your servant, and whoever wants to be first must be your slave just as the Son of Man did not come to be served, but to serve, and to give his life as a ransom for many."

esus said in Mark 8:35

"For whosoever will save his life shall lose it, but whosoever shall lose his life for my sake and the gospel's the same shall save it."

. Helping others makes you feel good

When you help others, it promotes positive physiological hanges in the brain associated with happiness. These rushes are ften followed by longer periods of calm and can eventually lead to etter wellbeing. Helping others improves social support, ncourages us to lead a more physically active lifestyle, distracts us rom our own problems, allows us to engage in a meaningful activity nd improves our self-esteem and competence.

. It brings a sense of belonging and reduces isolation

Being a part of a social network leads to a feeling of elonging. Face-to-face activities such as volunteering at a drop-in entre can help reduce loneliness and isolation.

. It helps to keep things in perspective

Many people do not realize the impact that a different erspective can have on their outlook on life. Helping others in times f need, especially those who are less privilege and fortunate than ourself, can provide a real sense of perspective and make you ealize how lucky you are, enabling you to stop focusing on what you eel you are missing - helping you to achieve a more positive outlook n the things that may be causing you stress.

4. It helps make the world a happier place – it is highly contagious.

Acts of kindness have the potential to make the world happier place. An act of kindness can improve confidence, control happiness and optimism. It can also encourage others to repeat the good deed they have experienced themselves. It contributes to a more positive community.

5. The more you do for others, the more you do for yourself

Evidence shows that the benefits of helping others can last long after the act itself by providing a 'kindness bank' of memories that can be drawn upon in the future.

PHYSICAL BENEFITS

1. It reduces stress

Doing things for others help maintain good health. Positive emotions reduce stress and boost our immune system, and in turn can protect us against disease.

2. It helps get rid of negative feelings

Negative emotions such as anger, aggression or hostility have a negative impact on our mind and body. Engaging in random acts of kindness can help decrease these feelings and stabilize our overall health.

3. It can help us live longer

Giving and helping others may increase our life span, this is because when we give unto others, we are bound to be happy and happiness increases our physical and psychological well-being. When you live and let others live, you are psychologically relieved and physically balance. You are also physically sound.

Studies of older people have shown that those who give
pport to others live longer than those who fail to do so. When
bitha was sick and died in the passage below. References were
ade to her good works by different types of people she had
ected and impacted positively; they insisted that she must not die.
e disciples sent for Peter to come to their aids. Invariable, God
bk control and she was brought back to life. Peradventure you die
lay, what will people say about you? How many people will stand
t to say you cannot just die like that, or will they be glad to say
ank God an obstruction has been removed. I pray God will speak
us in a better way.

t 9:36-39

*"Now there was at Joppa a certain disciple named
Tabitha, which by interpretation is called Dorcas: this
woman was full of good works and alms deeds which
she did. And it came to pass in those days, that she
was sick, and died:..... ...Then Peter arose and went
with them. When he was come, they brought him into
the upper chamber, and all the widows stood by him
weeping, and shewing the coats and garments which
Dorcas made , while she was with them. But Peter put
all forth, and kneeled...... Tabitha, arise. And she
opened her eyes: and when she saw Peter, she sat up"*

Chapter Six

Doing Good By Salvation

> **Be passionate about doing Good you are only loading your heaven as your rain is about to fall**

-Sola Olukoya-

The first "Do Good" means you must be Saved.

1. You must be born again. ***Romans 3:12***,
There is none that doeth good."

2. You can't save yourself. ***Titus 3:5,***
Not by works of righteousness (good works)   which we have done, but according to his mercy he saved us...."

3. "It is finished," ***John 19:30,*** Jesus has finished the work of our salvation by saying it is finished on the cross of Calvary. Salvation was finalized with Him on the cross. Jesus paid it all by shedding His blood on the cross of Calvary. A song says:
Jesus paid it all,
All to Him I owe.
Sin hath left a crimson stain,
He washed it white as snow."

Salvation is Essential. You will not be able to properly do good in the two other ways without getting saved first. Your first purpose in life is to get saved. Verse 29 is speaking of two kinds of people who have died and will be resurrected. First are those who have done good in relation to righteousness and are therefore saved.

The second are those who have done evil in relation to righteousness and are unsaved. Which kind of person are you? Have you done good in this way? Have you been saved? Salvation brings Resurrection. Notice what happens after the resurrection of life: There is Resurrection of life for the saved. There is Resurrection of damnation for the unsaved.

The Decision to "Do Good" (Accept His Righteousness) is yours. Some might say I will take my chances. Some might even say I'm going to wait a while. The Bible says don't put it off, for salvation through Christ is the only entrance to eternal life in heaven. Don't make the mistake of putting it off until it's too late.

Chapter Seven

Doing Good
By
Soul Winning

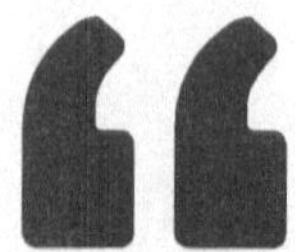

Keep Sowing
Keep Scattering
Keep Sending
Keep Spreading
Keep Scoring
Keep Soaring...

Sola Olukoya

Another means of doing good is by engaging in soul winning, we must be ready to go into the entire world, witnessing to the sinners about the love of God to the universe. We must be ready to go about like Jesus Christ our master doing good.

Acts 10:38

> *"How God anointed Jesus of Nazareth with the Holy Ghost and with power: who went about doing good, and healing all that were oppressed of the devil; for God was with him."*

In this verse of the scripture it was said that Jesus was going about "Doing Good." Does that mean that Jesus had to get saved? No, it means He went about saving people. So we are to seek the lost sheep and get the unsaved, saved.

Luke 19:10

> *"For the Son of Man is come to seek and to save that which was lost."*

Seeking and saving the lost is the act of doing good that we are emulate. Are we doing good in this area? If not we are committing sin.

James 4:17

> *"He that knoweth how to do good and doeth it not, to him it is sin."*

"Do good" here means to get those that are not saved, saved. Soul winning is a command. If we disobey this command, we may stop the supply of God's blessings to our lives.

Doing Good by Serving.
(Acts 10:38)

The latter part of this verse says, *"and healing all who were oppressed of the devil.* So we are to do good with Godly concern and care in the following ways.

1.   Jesus healed the sick. We must have concern for the si[ck]
        people around us. We can pray for them, take them to t[he]
        hospital and foot their hospital bills.
2.   He made the blind eyes see. Miracles can be done throug[h]
        our hands too.
3.   He fed the multitudes. We too can provide food for the nee[dy]
        and become the source of livelihood for the poor and t[he]
        oppressed around us. On and on, Jesus performed ma[ny]
        other miracles.
4.   *John 14:12* says, *"Greater works than these shall he (the believe[r])
        do. "*How do we accomplish this?

You must bathe yourself in the Bible.

1.   Jesus always healed with the Word.
        Psalm 107:20,
        *"He sent His Word and healed them and delivered them
        from their destruction."*
2.   It wasn't magic...it was His Word.
3.   You can't heal anyone yourself...you don't have the power [to]
        solve mental, physical or spiritual problems. But the Word [of]
        God has the power to do so. Do you know the Word? Do yo[u]
        study to show yourself, approved? Can you apply the healin[g]
        balm to a sick person? There is need for you to know the wo[rd]
        of God, by studying it every day.

You must pray.

1.   Private prayer. How much time do you spend in the place [of]
        prayer? If an emergency arose, could you get right int[o]
        heaven with your prayers? Do you have access to the power [of]
        God? If you haven't been praying, you don't. If you are n[ot]
        "prayed up" it will take time to confess your sin first and the[n]
        get to the heart of God.
2.   Intercessory prayer. You need to engage in intercesso[ry]
        prayers.

Luke 22:32,
"But I have prayed for these, that thy faith fail not...."

ou must live a Godly Life.

We must be immune against diseases ourselves, if we expect ɔ help the sick. Have you ever seen a discouraged person helping nother discouraged person? No one gets well that way. You ould't go to a dentist who has a mouth full of decaying teeth, ould you? No, it is impossible. It would be foolish to take cold edicine and stand out in the freezing cold rain all day. You will have ɔ live a Godly life , know the right word of God to apply for each ituation and be a prayer warrior, or else you will find it difficult elping those who come to our door pleading for help.

Chapter Eight

Life Is Not About Duration But Donation

**" Life is not
about duration
is about donation,
doing good does not
reduce you, It adds
value to your life."**

-Sola Olukoya-

ife is very short so you must make use of every opportunity God has given unto you to affect lives.

s not a matter if you think you are sowing or not. Step out of the eception and recognize that your life is one big field waiting for the ght seeds to be planted. It's best to take out a little time to do an ventory of your life. You can start with a small seed of etermination to make a change and one day reap a huge dividend eternal reward from God.

ebrews 11:6 KJV

But without faith it is impossible to please him : for he that cometh to God must believe that he is, and that he is a rewarder of them that diligently seek him.

Doing good, is one of the simplest, yet most ignored concepts life. Anything we put our time, energy, money, or focus on is an act doing good. When ever we sow good things we definitely reap od as the result. The ramification of our reaping depends on the mount of effort and time we put into the sowing. The Bible gives ery clear teaching on this reality that can influence our eternal wards. Let's look at the mystery behind sowing and reaping:

w Tears...Reap Joy

hose who sow with tears will reap with songs of joy" (Psalm 126:5) any times we go through unpleasant experiences whether due to agedies, disappointments, or sickness. Yet for those who put their ust in the Lord, there can still be peace and joy in the midst of —not because we don't hurt, but because God is with us. He ecomes our refuge and hope to get through the difficult days.

ow Righteousness...Reap Reward

wicked person earns deceptive wages, but the one who sows

righteousness reaps a sure reward" *(Proverbs 11:18).*
Doing the right thing doesn't always make us look good or fe
appreciated. Sometimes doing the righteous thing will make oth
people hate us. Our choice is about God—His glory and honor
evident in our right decisions. There's reward in this lifetime and th
next when we press ourselves to sow.

Sow Injustice...Reap Calamity

*"Whoever sows injustice reaps calamity, and the rod they wield in fury w
be broken" **(Proverbs 22:8).***
Nothing we do is hidden from the Lord. When we choose to act in a
unjust manner towards people we will reap calamity or pain from
eventually. Many of us don't recognize that sometimes we a
suffering indirectly for things we've done wrong. The Lord is patie
and wants each of His children to come to the place of dealing wi
injustice in our hearts and actions.

Sow to the Flesh/Spirit... Reap Destruction/Eternal Life

This is one of my favorite scripture,

> *"Do not be deceived: God cannot be mocked. A man
> reaps what he sows. Whoever sows to please their
> flesh, from the flesh will reap destruction; whoever
> sows to please the Spirit, from the Spirit will reap
> eternal life" **(Galatians 6:7-8).***

We can deceive ourselves into believing that we won't pay th
price for sowing into our flesh. However, God knows and He w
render due justice to each person on the earth. Destruction an
eternal life are complete opposites—if we want eternal life and w
need to take the correct actions of making the investment in
spiritual decisions and/or disciplines.

Sow Sparingly/Generously... Reap Sparingly/Generously

> *"Remember this: Whoever sows sparingly will also*

reap sparingly, and whoever sows generously will also reap generously" (2 Corinthians 9:6).

Stinginess and hoarding should never be a part of a christian's walk. We are called to hold lightly to material things as a means for essential life necessities. However many of us are guilty for sowing our money sparingly towards God's work, but generously towards our needs and/or wants. God pours out blessings on the faithful generous believers that are far more expansive than just money. He blesses with His presence filled with joy and peace in incredible generosity.

Sow Nothing...Reap Nothing

"Then another servant came and said, 'Sir, here is your mina; I have kept it laid away in a piece of cloth. I was afraid of you, because you are a hard man. You take out what you did not put in and reap what you did not sow" ***(Luke 19:20-21).***

At the judgment seat of Christ, there will be tears of regret for many believers. They will make it into heaven because of their faith in Jesus, yet they will suffer loss because they sowed nothing with what God gave them. We are saved by Christ to do good works for the kingdom. Good works is the doing good we are talking about. Believers must use their gifts given to them from God to affect change in their families and communities.

The money, houses, cloths, wealth, and what you have will not follow you to heaven.

The more you give the more God increases you. My life is a bundle of testimonies and I don't teach what I have not practiced.

Sow in good soil...Reap a Crop

"Jesus told them another parable: 'The kingdom of heaven is like a man who sowed good seed in his field"

(Matthew 13:24).
The man sowing is Jesus and the good seed are those who belong t
the kingdom of God. The Lord has planted His people specificall
where He can use their lives for God's glory. We are meant to shin
out of the worldly darkness with the light of Jesus Christ. Our word
actions, and attitudes reflect the beautiful transformation c
knowing God and being known by Him.

Start doing good today and you will never miss out in life.

20 Scriptures on Doing Good

Isaiah 3:10

Say ye to the righteous, that it shall be well with him; for they shall eat the fruit of their doings.

Psalm 37:3

> "Trust in the LORD and do good; dwell in the land and cultivate faithfulness."

Psalm 37:27

> "Depart from evil and do good, So you will abide forever."

Psalm 51:18

> "By Your favor do good to Zion; Build the walls of Jerusalem."

Isaiah 41:23

> "Declare the things that are going to come afterward, That we may know that you are gods; Indeed, do good or evil, that we may anxiously look about us and fear together."

Psalm 34:14

> "Depart from evil and do good; Seek peace and pursue it."

Proverbs 3:27

> "Do not withhold good from those to whom it is due, When it is in your power to do it."

Luke 6:35

> "But love your enemies, and do good, and lend, expecting nothing in return; and your reward will be great, and you will be sons of the Most High; for He Himself is kind to ungrateful and evil men."

Galatians 6:10

> "So then, while we have opportunity, let us do good to all people, and especially to those who are of the household of the faith."

Matthew 12:12

> "How much more valuable then is a man than a sheep! So then, it is lawful to do good on the Sabbath."

1 Thessalonians 5:15

"See that no one repays another with evil for evil, but always seek after that which is good for one another and for all people.

Thessalonians 3:13

"But as for you, brethren, do not grow weary of doing good.

Timothy 6:18

"Instruct them to do good, to be rich in good works, to be generous and ready to share"

Titus 3:1

"Remind them to be subject to rulers, to authorities, to be obedient, to be ready for every good deed"

Titus 3:8

"This is a trustworthy statement; and concerning these things I want you to speak confidently, so that those who have believed God will be careful to engage in good deeds. These things are good and profitable for men."

Hebrews 13:16

"And do not neglect doing good and sharing, for with such sacrifices God is pleased."

Peter 3:11

"He must turn away from evil and do good; he must seek peace pursue it"

Luke 6:27

"But I say to you who hear, love your enemies, do good to those who hate you"

Luke 6:33

"If you do good to those who do good to you, what credit is that to you? For even sinners do the same."

Luke 6:9

"And Jesus said to them, "I ask you, is it lawful to do good or to do harm on the Sabbath, to save a life or to destroy it?"

www.ingramcontent.com/pod-product-compliance
Lightning Source LLC
Chambersburg PA
CBHW020936160726
47993CB00007B/2806